# KIDS GET CODING

## CODING IN THE REAL WORLD

Heather Lyons

Illustrations by Alex Westgate & Dan Crisp

Lerner Publications ◆ Minneapolis

# Contents

Children will need access to the Internet for most of the activities in this book. Parents or teachers should supervise Internet use and discuss online safety with children.

# Getting Started

Hi! I'm Data Duck. I'm going to tell you about the computers that are all around us. We can't always see them, but they play a big part in our lives every day.

All around us, there are computers that control machines, vehicles, robots, lights, and many other things. They can do this because of the way they are programmed. When we program a computer, we tell it what to do using code.

## DATA DUCK

Code is a set of instructions we use to tell computers what to do. In this book, we will be using coding blocks like the ones below. Coding blocks are instructions that we can combine to create code for a computer.

Change height by -30 feet (-9 meters)

Play duck call

There are lots of activities in the book for you to try out. There are also some online activities for you to practice. For the online activities, go to **www.blueshiftcoding.com/kidsgetcoding** and look for the activity with the page number from the book.

# Everyday Computers

Did you know that computers aren't just in our homes and schools? They are around us almost all the time. Computers control the streetlights, our cars, and things such as lights and alarms in and around our homes.

Many of these computers around us include something called a sensor. Sensors can pick up on certain things around them. Some can measure the temperature. Others sense whether it is light or dark, and some can sense if there are any objects nearby.

**Streetlights:** A streetlight uses a light sensor to find out when it's getting dark. Once it is dark, the light turns on.

**Houses:** Some houses have a motion sensor outside that can find out if somebody is moving toward the house at night and turn on a light when the person gets close.

**Cars:** Some cars have distance sensors. These sensors find out how far away the car is from other objects. Drivers use these sensors when they are parking their cars.

## Lights On!

Some cars turn on their headlights when it gets dark outside.
Can you figure out which kind of sensor a car uses to do this?

A. A sensor that measures the distance between itself and other cars

B. A sensor that measures how light or dark it is outside

C. A sensor that measures the temperature outside

Turn to page 23 to see the answers.

**DATA DUCK**
Sensors are a bit like our senses! Do you remember what our senses are? Think of three senses and what they can do.

# Car or Computer?

Cars have many computers in them—some even have hundreds! These computers all make sure the car works the way it should.

There are computers that control the car's heating, its speed, and its lights. Some computers can show maps of the area the car is in while others can play music. Some cars have so many computers that they can even drive themselves!

## DATA DUCK

In a car, the sensors pass on the information they find out to the car's computer. This is called input. Then the computer passes signals to other parts of the car to tell them to do certain things. This is called output.

## Time for a Refill

Drivers need to know in good time when their car's gas tank needs refilling because they still need to be able to drive to the gas station. Look at the inputs and outputs below and pick which ones mean this car's computer is doing its job properly.

Turn to page 23 to see the answers.

### Input:

1. The tank sensor tells the computer that the tank is full.

2. The tank sensor tells the computer that the tank is empty.

3. The tank sensor tells the computer that the tank is almost empty.

### Output:

1. The computer passes on a signal to the warning light to start flashing.

2. The computer passes on a signal to the radio to play music.

3. The computer passes on a signal to the heater to switch on.

# Road Safety

Traffic lights are very important. They keep people who are crossing the street safe. They also keep traffic moving, so that we can all get to where we need to go. And they all work with sensors!

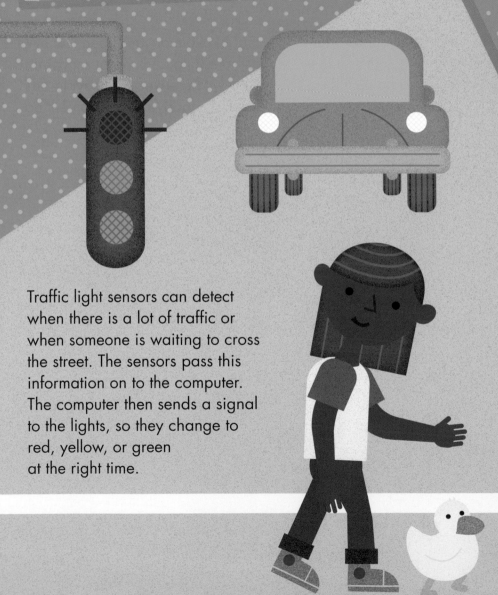

Traffic light sensors can detect when there is a lot of traffic or when someone is waiting to cross the street. The sensors pass this information on to the computer. The computer then sends a signal to the lights, so they change to red, yellow, or green at the right time.

**DATA DUCK**
It's very important for the traffic light's computer to change the lights at the right time. This helps everyone on the road stay safe.

## Change the Lights

Traffic light computers are programmed to make sure they pass on the right information to the lights. Have a look at the information below and choose which signals the computer needs to send to the lights.

Turn to page 23 to see the answers.

**Sensor information:** There are many people waiting to cross the road.

**Computer signal to lights:**

A: Turn red for cars. Then turn green for people, so they can cross.

B: Stay green for cars. Turn green for people too.

**Sensor information:** There are many cars waiting at a red light and not many people crossing the road.

**Computer signal to lights:**

A: First turn green for cars. Then turn red for people.

B: First turn red for people. Then turn green for cars.

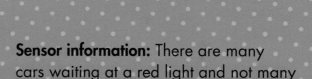

# Home Sweet Home

Computers in our homes help keep us safe and comfortable. They make sure our rooms aren't too cold, they tell us when there is a fire, and they switch on lights when it's dark outside.

**Alarm System:** Sensors tell a computer when a door or a window is opened. The computer sends a signal to switch on a loud alarm. Some computers even send a signal to the police, so they know there has been a break-in.

**Smoke Detector:** Sensors tell a computer when there is smoke in the house. The computer sets off an alarm to warn people that something is burning.

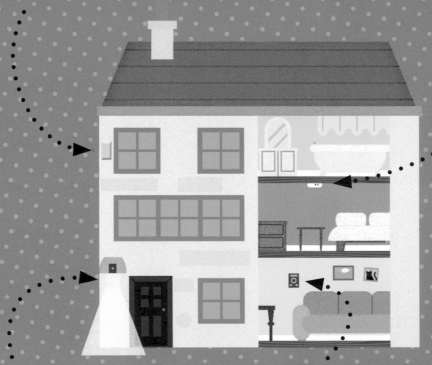

**Automatic Light:** A movement sensor tells a computer when someone is moving outside the house. The computer switches on the outside light.

**Thermostat:** This computer uses a temperature sensor to check whether rooms are too cold or warm. The computer then passes on the right signal to the heating system.

## Invent It!

Can you think of a computer you would like to invent for your house? What would it be able to do? Can you think of the sorts of sensors it might use? Draw your invention and explain how it would work.

## DATA DUCK

There are many other great inventions that can help around the home! There are mini robots that vacuum the floor in any room when it gets dirty, and devices that make sure plants get watered at the right time. All of these inventions use computers.

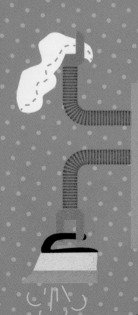

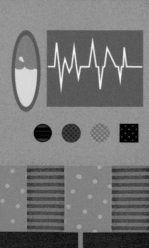

# Shopping

When we go to a store, computers keep track of what we buy and how much we pay. Most of the time, the computers find out all this information thanks to something called a bar code.

A bar code is a picture made up of lots of lines and numbers. You can find a bar code on the back of this book! Computers can read bar codes with the help of a sensor called a scanner. The bar codes help computers to find out what the scanned item is and how much it costs.

## DATA DUCK

At a store checkout, all the items a customer would like to buy are scanned. The information on the bar code is passed on from the scanner to a computer. The computer then adds up the cost of all the items and shows the amount on the screen.

## Time to Add Up

Imagine you are the checkout computer. Which total amount would you send to the screen if the scanner passed on this information:

Turn to page 23 to see the answers.

| | |
|---|---|
| cheese | $2 |
| fish | $3 |
| milk | $1 |
| bread | $1 |
| | |

# Money, Money

At store checkouts, we use scanners and computers to tell us how much we need to pay for our shopping. When we pay, we sometimes use even more computers!

People can pay for things by using a bank card or even their phone. They do this by tapping the phone or using the card with a small machine called a reader. Information is sent to and from the reader so that money goes from the person's bank account to pay the store.

## DATA DUCK

All computers need a battery or electricity to work. So the reader sends electric power to the bank card. This means that the card is powered and can now send and receive information.

# Payment Problems

Data Duck is at the store and wants to buy some eggs that cost $1.50. He puts his card in the reader but gets an error message and a beep. He can't pay with his card. What might have happened?

A.  He only has $1 left in his bank account.

B.  The machine can't connect to the bank.

C.  His card is cracked.

D.  Any of the above.

Turn to page 23 to see the answers.

# Flying High

Planes, helicopters, and even small flying robots called drones all need sensors and computers to fly. Without them, these aircraft wouldn't even be able to lift off the ground.

One of the most important sensors is the distance sensor, which can measure the distance between the aircraft and the ground. The pilot needs to know this information so that she can make sure the aircraft doesn't land too soon or crash.

## DATA DUCK

Aircraft sensors send their information to a computer. The computer then passes the information on to the dashboard, where the pilot can read it.

## Keep It Up!

Look at the coding blocks below and choose which one needs to sit in the gap so the drone never flies too high.

Turn to page 23 to see the answers.

If height is over 300 feet (91 m) then

Repeat until height is under 300 feet (91 m)

Play duck call

Change height by -30 feet (-9 m)

Turn to left

# Follow that Robot!

Robots are used for many things, from building cars to moving goods. Inside a robot, a computer is connected to sensors and motors. The motors make the robot move.

One kind of robot that uses sensors and motors to move around is called a line-following robot. It can follow a line on the ground. This is because there is a sensor at the bottom of the robot that can find out where the line is. The computer makes sure the robot follows the line as it moves around.

## DATA DUCK

We can program the computers inside these robots to do all sorts of amazing things. Some robots help doctors perform operations. Others can build cars or even play table tennis!

# Build a Robot!

Let's build our own robot! To help it work, we need to make sure our robot has an input and an output. Look at the list below and pick one of each. What will your robot be able to do?

**Input:**

1. Distance sensor—this can find out how far away objects are from the robot.

2. Light sensor—this can find out whether it is light or dark around the robot.

**Output:**

1. Motor attached to arms—this means our robot can do things such as flick a light switch.

2. Motor attached to wheels—this means our robot can move around.

# The Future

Computers are everywhere. They can be so tiny that we can barely see them. They can send information to each other and to devices such as phones without needing any wires.

These days we can even wear computers such as smart watches. These are watches with tiny computers in them that tell us things about ourselves. They can show us how fast we are breathing and how long we slept last night.

## DATA DUCK

We can also put computers inside the machines we use every day such as kettles and toasters! These machines can send and receive information from other computers. For example, we could use a phone to switch on the kettle!

## A Toast to Friends!

Someone has invented a toaster that sends a message to all your friends when you make a piece of toast! Now it's your turn. Think about what your toaster of the future might be able to do. Write down or draw your design.

# Extension Activities

Go to **blueshiftcoding.com/kidsgetcoding** for more fun activities and to practice

- using coding blocks
- writing programs
- predicting what programs will do
- exploring sensors

# Words to Remember

**code:** the arrangement of instructions in a computer program

**dashboard:** in cars and planes, a panel with controls and information that is fitted in front of the driver or pilot

**input:** something such as a sensor that puts information into a computer

**output:** something such as a warning light or an alarm used to send information out of a computer

**scanner:** a device that is used to read bar codes and send the information to a computer

**sensor:** a device that works like our senses and can measure light, temperature, and movement

# Activity Answers

## p. 5

B. A sensor that measures how light or dark it is outside sends a signal to the car's computer to turn on the headlights when it's dark.

## p. 7

Input:

3. The tank sensor tells the computer that the tank is nearly empty.

Output:

1. The computer passes on a signal to the warning light to start flashing.

## p. 9

Sensor information: There are many people waiting to cross the road.

Computer signal to lights:

A: Turn red for cars. Then turn green for people, so they can cross.

Sensor information: There are many cars waiting at a red light and not many people crossing the road.

Computer signal to lights:

B: First turn red for people. Then turn green for cars.

## p. 13

The computer would send the amount of $7 to the screen ($2 + $3 + $1 + $1 = $7).

## p. 15

D. Any of the above.

## p. 17

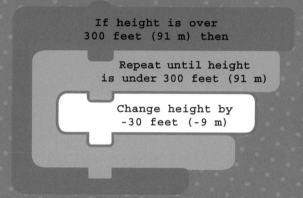

If height is over 300 feet (91 m) then

Repeat until height is under 300 feet (91 m)

Change height by -30 feet (-9 m)

# Index

First American edition published in 2018 by Lerner Publishing Group, Inc.
First published in Great Britain in 2017 by Wayland, an imprint of Hachette Children's Group
Copyright © Hodder & Stoughton, 2017
Text copyright © Heather Lyons

Lerner Publications Company
A division of Lerner Publishing Group, Inc.
241 First Avenue North
Minneapolis, MN 55401 USA

For reading levels and more information, look up this title at www.lernerbooks.com.

Main body text set in Futura Std. Book 12/16. Typeface provided by Adobe Systems.

**Library of Congress Cataloging-in-Publication Data**
Names: Lyons, Heather (Heather K.), author. | Westgate, Alex, illustrator. | Crisp, Dan, illustrator. | Lyons, Heather (Heather K.). Kids get coding.
Title: Coding in the real world / Heather Lyons ; illustrated by Alex Westgate and Dan Crisp.
Description: Minneapolis : Lerner Publications, [2017] | Series: Kids get coding | Includes index.
Identifiers: LCCN 2016052498 (print) | LCCN 2016058899 (ebook) | ISBN 9781512439434 (lb : alk. paper) | ISBN 9781512455861 (pb : alk. paper) | ISBN 9781512450538 (eb pdf)
Subjects: LCSH: Computer programming—Juvenile literature. | Information technology—Juvenile literature. | Technological innovations—Juvenile literature.
Classification: LCC QA/6.6 .L88525 2017 (print) | LCC QA76.6 (ebook) | DDC 005.1–dc23

LC record available at https://lccn.loc.gov/2016052498

Manufactured in the United States of America
2-44817-25429-9/26/2017